GIRL,
LET GO OR
BE DRAGGED

GIRL, LET GO OR BE DRAGGED

A Girlfriend's Guide to Not Getting Played or Playing Herself

Book I

SHENISE TRUESDELL

GIRL LET GO OR BE DRAGGED:
A Girlfriend's Guide to Not Getting Played or Playing Herself
Book I

Published by Behavior Etiquette Institute

ISBN (paperback): 979-8-9876857-0-9
eISBN: 979-8-9876857-1-6

To every woman who is learning
to put herself first

CONTENTS

PREFACE

It seems dating has progressively become more challenging. We log onto social media and see rants in statuses and comments about infidelity and lies as the leading complaints. I hear so many people from various walks of life—regardless of ethnicity, race, or gender—express similar concerns about the state of dating. Is it all a coincidence, or is this the new normal? Either way, it's alarming.

One can only question if the quality of people has collectively decreased, or is it that most people simply do not value committed relationships as much anymore. Whatever the case may be, it appears to be affecting many of us. Unfortunately, I was not exempt from this; the many includes me as well.

I'm often considered a nice person by others, and I must admit, "nice" is certainly a word I would have used to describe myself. It's part of the reason I became an etiquette consultant. However, it is this same niceness that has gotten me into unhealthy romantic situations more often than I'd care to admit. See, my niceness led me to give my past romantic partners the benefit of the doubt even when they didn't deserve it. This niceness was a more naive level of vulnerability that ultimately led to me being taken advantage of and sometimes outright played (Note: It is better to be kind than to be nice; kindness offers more realism and wisdom, while niceness is more guileless). This continued until I'd had enough and finally had that hard conversation with myself and God after noticing this pattern in my life. What I realized was the same niceness I was extending to everyone else, I needed to extend to myself first!

After this self-discovery, I wanted to make sure I was holding myself accountable for the poor decisions I had been making in my life. There was no way I could fully blame these men for playing me when I was the one who allowed it. Yes, you read right—I allowed it! As women, we often speak of how men may have done us wrong despite our being faithful and good to them. However, if we made healthier decisions regarding ourselves in those relationships, could that have been possible? The healthiest decision to make in these situations is to walk away at the first sight of toxicity. Now, I understand that some of us can't immediately leave a relationship for various reasons. However, I'm speaking to those of us who choose to stay when we don't necessarily have to. We have to incline our ear to listen to the voice of God and the nudging of our spirit when something is not divinely aligned. It's way past time we are kinder to ourselves by making healthier decisions in relationships. Sometimes we have to walk away from what's not healthily serving us; sometimes we have to simply let go, or be dragged!

ACKNOWLEDGMENTS

First and foremost, God, I thank You and acknowledge You in all Your ways. You have been more than good, and we know that all things work together for good for those who love God and are called according to His purpose. I'm thankful for the lessons and the blessings. You are so faithful, and I'm forever grateful.

Thank you, my Sun, Jahsiah, who single-handedly supported me with this project through long days and nights. I think of all the times I made you practice your writing skills with essays as a kid instead of playing video games, and how it has now come full circle to help me with my book. Pure awesomeness!

Thank you, Mom, for always having my back throughout my life decisions.

Thank you to the courageous women, who, in efforts to set other women free, allowed me to use your stories in this book project. I am most grateful to each of you!

Thanks to the women (too many to name!) who encouraged me on this journey and pushed me to keep going. Your words mattered.

Thank you to my failed attempts at forever. Whew! Without you it would be impossible for me to have the wisdom I possess today. Without you, I would not have been able to write this book. F.N.F.

INTRODUCTION

They say wisdom is knowledge applied. One of the best expressions of wisdom is learning from the experiences and faults of others to prevent making those same mistakes. This book is a collection of experiences of brave women from all walks of life who share their stories. Their experiences are meant to serve as that wisdom.

As a woman, society has trained me to put others first. As an etiquette consultant, I teach how to extend courtesy and kindness to others. Seldom has anyone encouraged me to extend that same courtesy and kindness to myself, so I had to do it. I'm now extending that permission to you.

Etiquette 101: Be Kind to You, First!

Matthew 22:39 tells us to love our neighbors as we love ourselves, and I believe that verse is a great representation of my Etiquette 101 theory. Furthermore, the question I ponder is, could we genuinely be kind to others if we are not first kind to ourselves?

Particularly, in romantic connections, we need to be kinder to ourselves by making healthier decisions. This book will help you understand some of the unhealthy choices you might be making in your relationships that may be putting you in a position to be taken advantage of. This guide will help you identify these choices and decide when it's time to let go or get dragged!

Note: *Aliases replace real names to conceal the identities of the brave women who shared their experiences in this book.*

She is soft, but I have made her strong;
You can't imagine what she can endure and overcome.
Even when she's been done wrong and has endured the unthinkable,
Her heart knows no contrition
Her love she still gives with no conditions
The most lovely and precious of all my creation,
So I gifted her with the spirit of insight and intuition

—SHENISE

1

DO NOT IGNORE YOUR INTUITION—IT IS YOUR GIFT FROM GAWD!

They say a woman's intuition can never steer her wrong, but how many of us trust ourselves enough to rely on our instincts for guidance?

We live in a logic-based society where endless information is at our fingertips, so if we make a claim, we have to back it up with facts. Therefore, since it's hard to prove intuition with science before the truth of a situation makes itself known, people don't take it as seriously as they should. Because our gut feelings are so often undervalued, it's easy to ignore them when something feels "off."

We owe it to ourselves to trust what we feel, or at least explore and inquire a bit more until that feeling is settled. This is not a green light to make wild accusations based on biased or desired outcomes. In fact, confronting people, especially our romantic partners, without having any type of evidence to substantiate our claims, is a recipe for anger and resentment. Instinct alone is never enough. At times, we might feel paranoid when feelings of uncertainty or insecurity arise, but when we understand that our makeup as human beings is more spiritual than physical, we stop ignoring when our gut tells our heart the truth. The more we practice using our intuition, the more comfortable we feel relying on it. It is a wise practice to utilize our intuition in all of our connections, but especially when it comes to romance. When we experience negative "vibes" in our romantic relationships, it's our responsibility to observe words and actions more keenly and ask pointed questions that will lead us to the answers we seek. When our bodies are communicating to us that something is not right, we need to trust this inherent protection.

Jeanette was dating a gentleman for a few months. One day he asked her to pack a bag and stay at his place for a few days, which wasn't out of the ordinary for them. She packed her bag, stayed over, and shared a wonderful evening with him on the first night. The next day, she drove him to work because his vehicle was out of commission, and then she went on to work herself. They spoke throughout the day as usual, and everything was going smoothly. The sun was shining, birds were chirping, and butterflies filled the Atlanta sky. As lunchtime approached, she thought about her beau and offered to pick up food for him since she had to run an errand near his job. He worked in luxury car sales, and they were in their busiest season, so he told her he was too busy to even have lunch and politely declined her offer.

After she finished her errand, she headed back to work. Jeanette was new to Atlanta and would often get lost, and since she only had an hour-long break, she wanted to be sure to get food and make it back on time. However, there was something strange about the drive back to work. She said something told her to go the direction opposite of where she needed to go, so she did. Suddenly, it was as if a force took over the car and was driving her, turn-by-turn. In nearly a daze, Jeanette repeatedly asked herself, "Where are you going, girl? Why are you driving toward this way?" She finally arrived in front of a place that was familiar to her. She immediately recognized the distinctive structure in the front of one of her favorite restaurants, the Atlanta Fish Market. Since she was already there, she decided to order her fave dish from there (sushi!) and hurry back to work.

Jeanette walked into the restaurant—excited to order her food—and proceeded to the bar to place her order, when she noticed a familiar bald head accompanied by a woman situated across from him in a booth. Surely her eyes were playing tricks on her, and at one point, she stretched her eyeballs to make sure she was seeing what she thought she was. Sadly, she was. Her beau, who was "too busy to even eat lunch," who she'd woken up beside that morning and shared a wonderful night with before, was on a date with another woman. She confronted him and confirmed that there was definitely infidelity taking place. Without trusting her intuition that day, there's no telling how long Jeanette would have remained tangled in her man's web of deception. She might have even ended up married and the mother of his child before learning he was a cheater. Jeanette chose to let go and not be dragged—she left that relationship!

Intuition, which is often referred to as our sixth sense, is a gift. Very rarely, if ever, will you hear a person say they wish they wouldn't have trusted what their gut was telling them. It's almost always the opposite: "I should have gone with my first mind. I should have trusted myself. I shouldn't have given the benefit of the doubt when I KNEW something was off." It's easy to say trust your intuition, but when it feels impossible for some of us to tap into it, there are some things to consider. According to Ivory Shields, a spiritual thought leader and holistic occupational therapist based in Atlanta, Georgia, one of the main reasons women don't trust their own intuition and inner voices is because we don't trust ourselves. She explains how we have been programmed at young ages to believe that sitting in stillness is equal to not being productive. We've been taught that meditation over prayer is demonic, when in fact it's a practice that allows us to become one with our intuition and inner voice. As a result, girls grow up to become women who can't even hear their inner voice and intuition, not to mention trusting it and allowing it to be a compass for navigating life's decisions and circumstances. Shields describes how one of the ways we can begin to strengthen the habit of listening to our intuition and inner voice is by taking the following steps, in this order:

- ◆ When faced with a decision, write it out.
- ◆ Write out the actual question we want answered.
- ◆ Write how we feel about the actual situation.
- ◆ Write what we think will be the outcome and how it makes us feel.

If we do this exercise often, we will start to recognize patterns. These patterns will show more favorable outcomes that align with our innate selves when we make decisions that are guided by our intuition, says Shields.

When it comes to major life decisions, especially those that involve someone else, we must make sure we're committing to situations that add life to us, not situations that steal life from us. If something feels off, it usually is. If we find it difficult to confront a significant other before we have all the concrete facts, we should weigh whether or not we feel comfortable enough with them to ask tough questions. We can approach hard conversations by posing questions such as, "I don't know if it's just me, but something in our relationship doesn't feel quite right. Is there anything we need to talk about?"

When all is said and done, we have a choice: We can live in misery knowing something isn't right and let it throw off our mental, physical, spiritual, and emotional health, or we can believe what the situation is telling us, trust our intuition, make hard choices, and sleep in peace at night. Whatever we choose, always remember that there is nothing wrong with putting ourselves first.

It is of popular belief that our intuition is simply God's voice within us. Psalm 16:7 says, "I will bless Yahweh, who has given me counsel." This is often interpreted as God's wise counsel being the Holy Spirit (inner voice) ministering to us and guiding us throughout life. Our obedience to the Spirit develops our ear to discern His guidance.

You are a rare beauty, indeed. Sculpted and handcrafted
by God for all to see—for all to see the beauty that lies
deep within because this beauty's journey of love, peace,
and acceptance breaks past the barriers of the surface skin,
and the light of her essence shines from deep within.
She doesn't have to chase after anyone,
especially because of whose she is, because in Him,
He has the perfect one—the one who will honor God, seek Him first,
and allow God to quench the fire of his thirst.
Allow the man to chase you because you are worth
the pursuit that goes far beyond surface compliments,
a charming smile, and external suits.
You are worth the chase because everyone doesn't have
the privilege to occupy the intimacy of your space.

—RM HARRIS

2

DON'T CHASE, BUT BE CHASED. STRAIGHT UP, NO CHASER!

We should never give a hard pursuit after someone. If they were equally interested in forming a significant relationship with us, we would not have to chase them in the first place. We should not always be readily available to our new partner, and they should not have immediate access to us at all times. We must keep some mystery about ourselves, but not so much as to create doubt in our partners. It is important that our new partners understand that we have a life of our own and are not just sitting around waiting for them. If we pace ourselves, that time apart will build anticipation, which will make it even more exciting when we unite. This creates somewhat of an idea of a chase. Be honest, it feels good to be chased a little, right?

As women, we want to be desired and adored, and we want someone to fight for us. We were created to be caressed and to be loved. We want to be told we are beautiful. For this reason, we should allow the man to pursue us and show us how he feels about us before we start giving him "wifey" benefits. However, if we are rejected, we must forgive ourselves for viewing someone's lack of reciprocation as a challenge or opportunity to convince them of our worth. Not being liked by everyone is a small consequence when we consider the overall reward of being liked by the right one! It is wise for us to rejoice in that moment instead of feeling rejected, because it is a step closer to Mr. Right!

According to Dr. LaTasha Russell, Doctor of Clinical Psychology and founder of Drive-By Therapy, what she has found in her private practice is that women who typically chase men are impatient and have a need to control. She mentions how, many times, subconsciously, when women take on the role of the pursuer, it is merely trying to take away the discomfort of vulnerability. She adds that the ultimate goal is to learn that vulnerability is a strength, and to be pursued is to know that you are desired.

If only we can trust wholeheartedly that what is meant for us is already ours, the better off we will be. We don't have to chase, nor do we have to beg the man who is truly for us. If we are unsure if we are giving a hard pursuit after our new partner, below are questions we should ask ourselves:

Are you the one initiating communication between you and your beau all the time? Does he call you, or are you the one who is always calling?

If you are making plans to visit your partner all the time, then how interested is he in spending time with you?

Does he romance you and take you on dates? If not, what is a romantic relationship without any, uhhh, romance?

Chasing a man (or anyone in any type of relationship for that matter!) is all bad. Below are a few points to consider about what may happen when we do:

- ◆ It's exhausting, detrimental to our self-esteem, and outright humiliating.
- ◆ If we have to chase him, ladies, here's the cold, hard truth: He may not want to be caught. A man who wants to be caught would not be running away.
- ◆ He may not be a "high-value" man or quality guy. Think about it. A man of character and integrity would be honest and upfront with us about his feelings and would never play games with our heart.
- ◆ Sometimes, we may be focusing so much of our energy on who is running away from us that we could be missing out on the prospects running toward us!
- ◆ Once we "catch" him, would we really want him? After the thrill of the chase is over, chances are we may realize he's not what we wanted after all. There is nothing worse than wasted effort or our most valuable asset—time!

Leigh was dating a guy who she liked so much. She would always call and text him. She often invited him into her home, and he would oblige every time! She, of course, would have liked for him to offer to come and see her ever so often instead of her asking all the time. This, of course, never happened. Leigh started to think about how she never really gave her guy an opportunity to make plans to see her or even ask her out on dates because she would always be the one to ask. So, she decided to scale back a little to allow him the space to take initiative. Unfortunately, he never did, and Leigh inadvertently discovered he may not have been that into her in the first place. She decided to let go, not be dragged, and moved on! After meeting another fellow and dating for about a month, guess who decided to reach out—old flame! After she had stopped giving the old flame so much attention, he then began pursuing her. Leigh wondered if she had pulled back and had not been so readily available in the beginning, would things have been different between the two of them. The truth is, it probably would have, but she held on to the truth that what is meant for her is meant for her.

The things women desire in a relationship should most certainly be considered, especially if it is bare minimum. In this case, Leigh honestly desired for her guy to basically take initiative and make plans to spend time with her. That is not asking for too much. If in any situation our guy is so elusive to the point that the most minuscule of things are too demanding, then we need to consider that he may not be our guy. Additionally, we must not internalize that, as we often do. We usually make it about us and may feed ourselves the false narrative that we are asking for too much, are unlovable, or are unworthy, when really it is just a matter of incompatibility. He simply may not be able to give love at the capacity we require. I say require because we require to be loved a certain way to show up as our best selves in the relationship. If that is not happening, then we simply can't afford to stay involved.

Never give a hard pursuit after someone who's basically showing disinterest. The plans God has for us are by far greater; therefore, we should never desperately chase after what essentially is not meant for us in the first place. The Bible says in 1 Corinthians 2:9, "But as it is written, Eye hath not seen, nor ear heard, neither have entered into the heart of man, the things which God hath prepared for them that love him." It is written that we can't even begin to imagine the greatness He has for our future.

You may not have been taught much about
personal boundaries and that's ok;
it isn't anything you can't learn along the way.
Along the way to a healthier you
Along the way to a kinder you
Because a kinder you, to you, is overdue
Love on you, first, and you may then have a healthier
relationship with a boo.

—SHENISE

3

EXTEND COURTESY TO YOURSELF. IN THE BEGINNING OF YOUR RELATIONSHIP, SET AND STAY FIRM ON PERSONAL BOUNDARIES.

It is essential to set personal boundaries in order to have healthy relationships of any type. Personal boundaries are important because they create the basic guidelines of how we desire to be treated; this is especially important when we are establishing romantic relationships.

Early on in our romantic relationships, we have the tendency to become so entangled with our new partners that we set little to no personal boundaries. *¡No bueno!* The early stage of a relationship is considered the infatuation stage, which can be very intense and outright amazing all at the same time! Don't that thang be goodt at the beginning?!? It could almost leave us feeling as if we are the only two people on earth and wanting to spend every minute of every day with our new boo. Let's be honest, it is quite natural for us to want to spend a lot of time together when it is new. However, this stage doesn't last forever, and it is unhealthy for us to try and extend it for the entirety of the relationship (although we often try!).

The infatuation stage is the most critical stage in a relationship because we must set boundaries, be very assertive of the boundaries we've set, and be attentive to our new boo's behaviors during this time. We are typically in bliss and mostly focused on extending the euphoric feeling of this stage instead of being observant to not miss very important "red flags."

To help combat being taken advantage of, or outright played, try not to become so ensnared with your new partner so early on. Things could get really "foggy," and it's usually very difficult trying to reinforce boundaries after this point. It is imperative to have your own life. Keep your own set of friends and outside interests as well. Girl, you know how you act when you get a new man. *side eye* Never cancel plans with friends or social engagements for the sake of your new relationship. This helps keep things healthy and well-balanced, and it gives you nearly hawk-eye vision to not miss any warning signs in your new relationship.

Personal boundaries are basic guidelines we create to establish how others are able to treat us and behave around us. Essentially, they constitute what behavior is acceptable and unacceptable to us. It would be naive of us to assume that every guy we date will always respect our boundaries, so it is important that we are prepared to respond in the event they overstep our boundaries. Enforcing consequences is just as important as actually establishing boundaries because it lets the guy know that not respecting our boundaries will not be tolerated. This is how we inadvertently teach them how to respect and treat us.

I know! I know! Being assertive can be uncomfortable and may sometimes come across as being mean, and let's face it—who wants to be the mean girl? Most of us want to always be muah-muah, kissy-kissy, and lovey-dovey with our beaus. I get it! However, while being courteous or kind to them (and others) is important, it is also important to extend that same level of consideration to ourselves first! You see, setting personal boundaries is the greatest form of kindness we could ever extend to ourselves. It is a notable expression of self-love when we put forth effort to ensure we are fostering the healthy connections we deserve. I will take it a step further and say that extending kindness to ourselves is the epitome of self-love. After interviewing a woman by the name of Vivi, I was able to see examples of just that, and how implementing personal boundaries early in a relationship can forfeit unnecessary hurt, pain, and wasted time.

Vivi talked about a gentleman she'd met one evening while dining alone at Cheesecake Factory's bar at Perimeter Mall. She described the encounter with the gentleman as a very pleasant one. She'd even gone on to mention how romantic sparks between the two had begun almost immediately! So, it is safe to say that Vivi was completely smitten over this gentleman. You see, Vivi is about a year and a half out of a very abusive, toxic, tumultuous, and volatile (Yes, all that!) relationship. After doing all the necessary self-work, Vivi was more than ready to re-enter the dating world. She is very intentional about fostering healthy romantic connections, so it was essential for her to implement personal boundaries as well as create a list of "rights to a healthy relationship" to help guide her. Vivi's list is shared at the end of this chapter.

Vivi explained that after three weeks of dating and being inseparable from her new guy, things were moving pretty fast. Although things were seemingly going well, there were a few concerns she had that made her realize she needed to slow things down. She noticed that every time she and her new guy would speak over the phone, it was always while he was out. In fact, she could only recall a few occurrences of speaking with him while he was inside his home, but each time, he was actually in the bathroom. In the past, Vivi would have probably ignored something like this and most certainly would not have addressed it, but not the new Vivi. She shared with him her observations, and he reassured her it was all in her head, and certainly they'd spoken many times while he was inside of his home. However, Vivi was very adamant they hadn't and stuck to her guns. She explained to him that her observation made her feel uneasy and gave the impression there was a reason he couldn't communicate with her while he was inside his home (or at least not while he's using the john!).

With all the self-work Vivi had done, she was determined not to fold. She made sure he understood her boundaries, and that in order for them to grow in a healthy relationship, intimate communication in the comfort and privacy of his home had to occur, and if not, it would compromise the chances of their relationship progressing. Still trying to convince Vivi it was all in her head, he then promised her that every evening, they'd speak right before bedtime. Needless to say, he was conveniently never available to speak in the evenings as he had promised, so Vivi ceased all communication between them. About a week later, Vivi received a random call from a woman demanding to know who'd been calling her fiancé from that telephone number for the past month. Turns out, Vivi's new guy was this woman's fiancé. Apparently, they lived together with their 2.5 children and had been together for ten years. If Vivi hadn't been assertive and firm on her boundaries, she would've proceeded with investing energy, feelings, and time into this relationship and ultimately getting played in the end. Vivi made the choice to let go before she got dragged!

Therefore, we have to know how to establish healthy emotional, physical, and psychological boundaries with our partners that will allow us to feel respected and valued. How? The first step is knowing your rights for a healthy relationship.

VIVI'S LIST OF RIGHTS
TO A HEALTHY RELATIONSHIP

We have the right:

◆ To feel safe in our relationships

....

◆ To have our boundaries and privacy respected

....

◆ To be heard and understood

....

◆ To feel validated

....

◆ To be appreciated and valued

....

◆ To say "no" and still be respected

....

◆ To have our needs and reasonable wants met

....

◆ To be treated respectfully

....

◆ To not be emotionally, physically, or verbally abused

....

◆ To "me time"

If you or someone you know has challenges in this area and needs help with establishing healthy boundaries and practicing assertiveness, please consider counseling or a therapist for guidance.

Extending courtesy to ourselves, or simply being kind to ourselves by setting boundaries and making healthier decisions in our relationships, is the utmost form of self-love. What the Bible tells us in 1 Corinthians 13 is, "If I give all I possess to the poor and give over my body to hardship that I may boast, but do not have love, I gain nothing." If we are so giving of ourselves to people just for the sake of saying we are in a relationship, really, what is there to gain? How is that healthy?

*He loves me, he loves me not, he loves me . . . but did
he earn this precious spot—the priceless spot of having
access to the intimacies of my heart because he should have been
earning this privilege from the very start.
Does he know you, and do you know him, or did you simply throw
caution to the wind just for the sake of it being
said that a relationship is what you're in.
So, I choose to keep my options open and not settle
too quickly—I'm looking for exclusivity but not at the expense of
rushing into it prematurely. I will take my time on this journey of
love because every good and perfect gift cometh down
from our heavenly Father above.*

—RM HARRIS

4

KEEP YOUR OPTIONS OPEN, AND DON'T SETTLE TOO QUICKLY. EXCLUSIVITY TO YOU HAS TO BE EARNED.

Few things bring greater regret than diving into something too fast thinking it's what's best, only to realize that had you waited, you could have saved yourself immeasurable heartache. Relationships are among the clearest examples of this.

We've all seen movies that celebrate whirlwind romances or heard stories of couples who laid eyes on each other and married a mere six weeks later, without realizing such stories are the slim minority. For most of us, time is our best friend. It will reveal what we need to know if we let it do its work. If you're wondering whether you're the one in the slim minority of instances of love at first sight, you're not. Let time tell you what you need to know instead.

Two concepts should be top-of-mind when considering how quickly to move forward in a relationship. First is the matter of significance. How do we know if someone is worth becoming significant in our life if we haven't taken the time to really get to know them? Second is the concept of exclusivity. How much do we truly value ourselves if we give exclusivity to someone we barely know?

A little experience will reveal whether they're deserving of us or not. Give sufficient time to watch him and test if he measures up to the standards you've set for someone who intends to enter and shake up your life. If the goal is a healthy, committed, long-term relationship, a smart practice is for us to establish a vetting process through which others prove their worthiness of our devotion, time, attention, and trust. Doing so is a sign of self-worth. Besides, jumping into the relationship that's most accessible might cause us to miss out on the relationship that's most suitable. You might be wondering, if that's the case, why do so many women do it? Why do so many women dive into relationships headfirst without considering all the potential outcomes? For most of us, the reasons fall into one of two categories:

◆ **We're afraid it will take too long to find someone new.**
When we're with a guy who knows all our flaws and still accepts us, who's met all our friends and family, and who can get on board with our hopes and dreams, we've probably got a winner. He likes us. He chooses us and isn't looking for anyone else, no matter how attractive others may be, and that kind of commitment is hard to come by. Therefore, when a man dedicates himself to us, we might feel like it would be foolish to let go. Maybe we had to go through a lot of rejection before finding someone who would treat us well. Maybe we believe there's no one else out there who'll adore us the same way, especially if we grew up with people

telling us there were only a few good men left. It's easy to convince ourselves that even if we don't reciprocate their feelings, we better hold on to what seems good because this is as good as it gets. Believing this causes us to stay and settle.

◆ **We're afraid of being alone.**

He's probably a nice guy. He probably wants to please us and might even think we're out of his league, so he goes out of his way to try to prove he's worthy. But listen when I tell you: Having no relationship at all is a better situation than being in one you've settled for. If we're not in it for the same reasons he is, we will be miserable. We'll always wonder what things could have been like had we walked away— how much further ahead we could have gotten in life, the places we could have gone, or simply the peace and contentment we could have experienced. If we relent to "good enough," we'll cause pain for everyone involved.

Sometimes, we settle for relationships because we feel like "it's time." This timeline might be determined by age, what our friends are doing in their relationships, or the desire to settle into a relationship we can grow old in. None of these factors will be enough to sustain us if we opt for someone who's only satisfactory. None of those daydreams will come to fruition because they will be tainted by longing and regret. If we're not sure when the right time is to settle down, we should consider if this is a person we'd want to build with, go through rough times with, go through the best of times with, and grow old with. If we're willing to date this person exclusively and cut off communication with anyone else we've been giving time and attention to, we may be ready to enter into an exclusive relationship in which both parties have verbally solidified and consciously decided to commit solely to each other. Still unsure? Consider the following as more signs of long-term relationship readiness:

◆ You prioritize his needs over your own. You no longer "look out for number one."
◆ You open up to each other in ways you've not done with anyone else.
◆ You do not allow petty arguments and quarrels to rock your relationship.
◆ You've met each other's families, friends, and loved ones and feel comfortable and accepted.
◆ You've lost interest in seeing anyone else.
◆ Your relationship has a deep emotional element that goes beyond sex.
◆ You're comfortable enough to be yourselves around each other.
◆ You talk about future plans with each other.
◆ You fret at the thought of losing each other.
◆ You can honestly say that you trust each other.

Exclusivity in a relationship is a big step. The more involved we get, the more invested we feel, and the harder it will be to walk away later. To save ourselves headaches and heartache, we must be selective about who we move into sacred territory with in the first place. Remember, if we take our time on the front end, we might be preserving our resources, peace, and sanity on the back end. There's no need to rush into anything, and if we deprive ourselves of the chance to explore our love lives to the fullest because someone treats us nicely, we're cheating ourselves. Remember, "If you rush it, you will ruin it. Pause, pray, and be patient."

Keep your options open and don't settle too quickly. Exclusivity to you has to be earned!

What does God say about waiting on Him and, umm, something about patience?!? Wait on God; moving prematurely may forfeit more suitable partners for us. Psalm 37:7 says, "Be still before the LORD and wait patiently for him." Wait on Him.

Communication is key to unlocking the imprisoned heart.
Whether in words, deeds, or actions, we must be careful because
the heart can be fractured from the very start.
Actions speak louder than words and every action is a verb that
yields a harvest to the only one that heard—the only one that heard
the frequency of lies that could not be fulfilled and penetrated
their souls and as a result they are ill.
So, pay close attention to not only what is said but more to what
an individual has done because this will reveal the truth—and from
it you cannot run, you must stand firm and flat-footed and say that
you will not participate in this masquerade.

—RM HARRIS

5

BELIEVE ACTIONS, NOT WORDS. PERIOD.

We are social creatures who are constantly on the hunt for fulfilling relationships, and this is from the moment we are born. In fact, scientists say babies who are left alone after birth can die from lack of attention and touch, and those who fail to bond with their parents can experience lifelong repercussions, including, but not limited to, mistrust of loved ones. We are built to trust, so when someone does not follow through on their word, it can be devastating— especially when it's Bae! Unfortunately, not everyone has good intentions. People can use our natural propensities against us for their own benefit. So how are we supposed to know when someone is playing us and whether or not they deserve our trust? Glad you've asked! Fortunately, this may be accomplished by simply having patience and honesty with ourselves first, and also understanding how relationships evolve so that we are not blindsided or taken off guard when our partner's words are not backed by action (i.e., when he's lying!).

Have you ever trusted the word of someone else only to discover it was betrayal? It is hurtful, and certainly an unpleasant feeling. We've all been there at least once, and some more often than we'd like to admit! Once we get past the infatuation phase and start to get attached, feelings of discomfort might overtake us. Once we've started to give away our trust, loosen boundaries, and let down defenses, it all might end in heartache. But maybe, just maybe, we have more to gain than to lose, and thinking about what we could gain feels better than worrying about what we might lose, right? That's why it's easier to give in than to let go. And how do we give in? By continuing to give them our trust.

According to Dr. LaTasha Russell, Doctor of Clinical Psychology and founder of Drive-By Therapy, the first word that comes to her mind when it comes to the subject is "denial." She notes that denial is a place where some women decide to live and not just visit and that clinically speaking, to most, denial feels safer than believing the truth. Dr. Russell explains that really looking at a man whose actions do not align with his words is difficult and that many times, out of desperation, we truly do not want to believe whatever he is saying to be "all talk." She believes that what is the most unfortunate truth about denial is that we are actually choosing to not see what is in front of us. She describes that with some of her female patients, some of the relationships that they had experienced would have never happened if they simply stopped to "listen to what he was doing." Her advice on the matter is, in the beginning of a relationship or while dating, to ask ourselves, "How gullible have I been?" and that our gut will tell us the answer.

Ladies, at this point, logic and emotion usually begin to battle. The old adage, "Actions speak louder than words," is pushed to the side. We want them to tell us what we want to hear, to prove to us that we are not wasting our time, that they're worth the hassle, and we'll get a return on our investment of energy into this relationship. But the truth is it's our responsibility to open our eyes and believe what's right in front of us. Marvin Gaye said, "Believe half of what you see and none of what you hear." Character is what a person does, not what a person says. If we feel something is off, and especially if they give us proof because their actions don't correspond with their declarations, we need to trust what's happening. If unacceptable behavior becomes a pattern, it's time for some hard decisions. Do we really want to pursue a relationship with someone who is showing us they can't be trusted? Or should we let go or be dragged? Cutting things off at this juncture might hurt, but that pain is nothing compared to what's coming if we don't take heed.

Let's be honest, ladies: When we get played, it's not always just our partner's fault. It often happens because we simply fall in love with potential instead of proof. Words are just sounds; they mean nothing without actions behind them. As human beings, words are our simplest form of communication that can be easily manipulated. If we rely on verbal communication too much and fall in love with words, we lose focus on what's important—actions. Actions are from the heart. They require sustained effort, and because they take more energy to execute, we can generally get more truth from actions than we can with just words. Words are cheap; actions are an investment. Yes, they can turn out to be fake too, but once the excitement wears off, what's real will prevail. We often hear people in long-term relationships or marriages say their partner changed once things went to the next level, and it's probably true. Both parties do it to a certain degree because we get comfortable. If our partner has said this about us in a disapproving manner, we should ask ourselves if it was because we simply stopped tolerating dishonesty and started speaking up more than we did in the beginning. Remember, no one likes to be called out for their inconsistent behaviors, especially when we have facts that contradict their words.

Now, because none of us are perfect, we cannot expect perfection from others. People are going to mess up or fall short. It's a given. What matters is what happens after the mess-up. If our partner apologizes but doesn't change his behavior, then I believe we may have our answer. We can now consider the possibility that our partner may not value us enough to feel we are deserving of that change. An apology is a promise that the offensive behavior will cease. While in some cases the change might take some time, there still needs to be proof of movement in the right direction. Are they making an earnest attempt, or do they just keep apologizing with no change in sight? Our forgiveness does not have to be unlimited, but it should certainly never be blind.

We tend to give people the benefit of the doubt when we probably should not. How many times have we gotten driving directions from a total stranger and considered whether they were telling us the truth or not? Exactly! We almost never question driving directions from strangers. It is imperative we pay attention to patterns and inconsistencies. There is a saying that when we meet someone new, we are only meeting their "representative." Once they've won us over and gotten comfortable, however, they will call the representative off duty and revert to the real them. No one can keep up their marketing forever and go on pretending to be someone or something they are not. When that happens, we realize we may have been ignoring the warning signs all along and that there is really no one else to blame except for ourselves. I know it is not comforting knowing we are the cause of our own pain, but it is important for us to remember to extend ourselves grace when things like this happen and to be gentle with ourselves. Take it as an opportunity of learning a very valuable lesson. We must pay attention to red flags so that we may use them as a compass now instead of regrets later. We should not easily take the word of someone without some sort of vetting process.

The bottom line is we should not always take people at their word. Instead, we should consider allowing them to prove their word is actually good before giving them full and total trust. We want to trust our new beau and believe things can work out, but we also don't want to be let down again, so we guard our hearts. The best and healthiest way to do this is to be honest with ourselves about what we want and refuse to compromise on the promises that we have made to ourselves. Repetitive misconduct is a character flaw that we should not stick around for.

We must always keep in mind that people are what they do, not what they say. Words are from the lips; actions are from the heart. Words can be comforting, but actions, they feel even better! Believe actions and not words.

If faith without works is dead, then words without action are—dead. This is precisely what the Bible says in James 2:14, "What does it profit, my brethren, if someone says he has faith, but does not have works?" It's all in the work—not the word.

Wherever there's smoke there's fire, they say,
But how solid is the word of they
Hearsay is gossip but gossip can be true
However, does the word of a loved one always bear truth
But then again, it all depends on who

—SHENISE

6

WHAT DO HIS FAMILY AND FRIENDS SAY ABOUT HIM, EVEN IN A JOKING MANNER? THERE'S 10% TRUTH IN EVERY "I'M JUST KIDDING."

You've met the man you've been waiting for. He's smart, funny, and attentive. He listens to your future hopes as well as your work frustrations, and he's memorized your favorite meals at your favorite restaurants. You've tried to be careful about giving your heart away too fast, but you can't help the daydreams of a thriving life together. Then the moment comes: He wants to introduce you to his family and close friends. You're in there, girl. Now it's just a matter of time.

Men don't introduce their inner circle to just anybody. You wonder what he's told them about you, but listen to me when I say you need to be even more concerned about what they're going to tell you about him.

When you walk into your love's family home, you'll be stepping into the place where he likely feels most comfortable. Anticipation and excitement will fill the air. People will get free with their tongues and excited about your future together. This is great for you. It means they'll be ready to dish information that nobody but his family could reveal. It's important to pay close attention, ask the right questions, and analyze the responses to keep yourself from future avoidable heartache.

His family will give you key insight into the person you haven't met yet. Let me be clear: Most people aren't faking at the start of a relationship; you likely just haven't been through enough to see the worst of them. Some folks see this as false advertising, but all of us—ALL of us—put our best foot forward at the start of a love affair to get the other person to like us as much as we like them. You know how people say their loved ones changed after marriage or a few years together? They didn't change; they just got comfortable. How can you avoid those unpleasant surprises? How he interacts with his family will give you clues.

Everybody loves a good story, right? And stories about your beau as a kid or teen will flow like wine during your first meeting. What was his favorite thing to do as a kid? How did he spend his extra time? How did he spend his time in college? Family and friends will be itching to tell you about his past antics, and inevitably, somebody will slip up and reveal a moment that isn't so shiny. Those comments should get your antennae up. Those are the red flags. How was he during a time when he got the angriest? Did he get in fights a lot? Why, and who started them? As you're listening to these stories, notice if anyone says something curious only to backpedal with a "Just kidding!" Listen, research tells us there is at least 10% truth in every "just kidding." When you hear something questionable, put it in your back pocket so you know what to ask him later, then pay attention to his responses and body language when he answers.

Learning how he was during his formative years will tell you why he is the way he is as an adult. Yes, people change and grow, but the past plays a big part of who they are today. You're going to want to know if he did things like harm animals, which is indicative of psychopathy. You'll want to know if he was always in trouble at school, because that might speak to what he thinks about authority. Did he study hard? Take summer jobs? Clean up around the house? Those are clues about his thoughts about carrying his weight, which you certainly want to be sure about before you make any long-term commitments. If he struggled with mental health issues or abuse, find out what lengths he's gone through to heal, as those experiences will certainly affect you intimately. People who don't heal their wounds bleed on those who didn't cut them, and you want to stay as clean as possible.

You may not learn everything the first time you meet the family, but if you meet them more than once, take opportunities to ask deeper questions. For example, it's important to know how he channels his feelings. As a child, did he punch holes in the wall? Break things? Hurt his sibling? Cry nonstop? Was he violent in any way? Everything is rainbows and roses during the infatuation phase, but one day, you will be mad at each other. I know it's hard to believe, but it's true. The warm fuzzies will wear off and real life will begin. You want a partner who will endure the hardships with you, not make them more difficult because he can't control his emotions.

While you're listening to his family, observe what they're like on their own and around him. Are they affectionate toward each other, or are they cold? Does there seem to be friction between anyone? Pay attention to how his parents interact with each other, or if they do at all. Whether we like it or not, to some degree, we mimic the patterns we watched in our formative years. Our relationships might not be a full reflection of our parents', but their dynamics will at least account for drops in the puddle.

Now, let's talk about his friends. His boys might not be as open with information as his family, but you can still get what you need. Watch their eyes and body language when the topic of women and relationships comes up. Those things say it all when you can't gather much from their words. On the other hand, some guys are wide open, so if they say something that makes you feel uneasy, take them at their word. Believe what they're telling you, even when they're not explicit.

For example, do they have a suggestive nickname for him, like Lady Slayer or Don Juan? Make it your business to find out why that is. How has he treated previous partners? The past can be a strong predictor of the future. If he's spent his life playing the field, don't think he'll magically hang up his cleats because he met you. As for his attitude under pressure, notice if they joke about his temper, fights he's had out in public, or raising his voice at other people. Understand this: If someone else can push him to a limit, you can too.

And finally, the adage, "Birds of a feather flock together," is cliché for a reason. When you look at your man, you're looking at the average of his friends. Pay attention to the vibe you get around them. Ask them what they do for a living, what they do for fun, and how they know each other. Ask questions about their favorite times together or anything else you can think of to help connect dots that reveal more about who he is. His friends are a mirror of his character, just like your friends are a mirror of yours.

Once the visits are over, you should have a decent amount of evidence to help you determine if you want to keep moving forward in a healthy relationship, if you need to take a step back and assess the situation, or if you need to sprint in the opposite direction. Whatever insight you gather, it's your responsibility for your sanity, your peace, and your future to believe it.

Cindy dodged a complete bullet by simply paying attention when visiting her beau's loved ones. What she discovered was enough to make your jaw drop. She and her beau traveled from Atlanta, Georgia, to Birmingham, Alabama, to spend Christmas with his family. As excited as she was to meet his family and friends, she was also very nervous about if they'd like her and what she might learn of him from his loved ones. See, they were in a fairly new relationship, and she sought to do her due diligence to ensure he really was "the one." If the family checked out, that would be reassurance of a healthy upbringing.

They arrived at his family's house and were immediately greeted as they parked. A very traditional Southern family, everyone was so happy at their arrival and were all waiting for them outside. *What a lovely family*, she thought to herself. Everyone appeared to be very well-balanced. They enjoyed dinner and sat around and talked about old times, and as the day reared, the mom tasked her beau with taking a few family members home before leaving to drive back to Atlanta. Cindy stayed at the house with the mom so there would be more space in the car for those he was driving home, but she did notice he didn't appear to be very comfortable with her staying—it was all over his facial expression. So, she was there alone with his mother and sister who, at one point, shared a moment of awkward silence with her. The mom proceeds to ask "So, how is he?" as the sister stared at her. Cindy was quite puzzled by the question and said, "Oh, he's fine." The mom and sister both asked if he shared any emotions at all and if he displayed any erratic behavior. By this time, Cindy was extremely uncomfortable because she realized the mom may have orchestrated time alone to disclose something to her. Well, unfortunately, she did, and it certainly wasn't anything Cindy could have ever imagined. Turns out, her beau suffered from personality disorders that made him dangerously violent. In fact, he'd been committed a few times in the past for it. Nothing could have prepared her for what she learned about the man she was falling madly in love with. She said it was a Christmas she'd never forget—the perfect gift! Had she not known of this, her life may have been in danger. So, she made the hard choice to let go and not be dragged by ending the relationship. Of course, she never spoke a word to him of what his family had disclosed to her.

Shonie had a very similar story. She went home with her beau for the holidays and also learned the unimaginable. Shonie had been dating her beau for nearly one year, so she was well acquainted with his immediate family. This particular holiday, one of her beau's cousins, who Shonie had never met, was there. The cousin seemed very cool and down to earth; in fact, she and Shonie had become fairly close within that short period of time. One thing about Shonie's beau's family—they drink! Everyone was a-feeling the moonshine that day, including the cousin. As Shonie and the cousin were conversing, the cousin inquired about how Shonie and her beau met. She then followed with a comment, "I'm surprised he even brought a woman home." Obviously, this statement would leave anyone curious, so Shonie proceeded to ask the cousin what she meant by that. After swearing Shonie into secrecy, she then shared information about a lover Shonie's beau had had for many years. A lover who was well-off financially, a lover who was very much married, but married with a wife and kids. Shonie knew immediately who the cousin was speaking of and that there could be some truth to what the cousin was saying, because she'd had her own suspicions of her beau's relationship with this gentleman, especially after he funded her beau's entire logistics business as a gift. In addition to that, this friend was always generous with her beau and never seemed to ask for anything back. This dared the question of whether her beau had a male lover who took care of him financially, which was more than likely true. Needless to say, she left him. Had Shonie not been attentively listening to her man's cousin, she may have never known this information.

When we are getting to know someone, being alert and attentive while in their presence is pivotal during this phase, especially when meeting their loved ones. It is wise to pay attention to EVERY word spoken. The Bible notes the importance of attentiveness in Proverbs 2:2, stating, "Make your ear attentive to wisdom, incline your heart to understanding."

I am fearfully and wonderfully made; I have lips, hips,
and fingertips as the deed, topped with attitude and soul
to help me reach any one of my goals.
All you can see is the external beautified portrait of me,
but the real me owns no color but is full of color, has wings to fly
and is more free than the mocha skin I'm wrapped in.
My legs are sandy sculptured pillars with roots reaching as far as
the tip of my sturdy brick feet—but will not open wide to receive
you before it's time to meet. Because my love is laced with every
trace of my thighs that you can only preview me with your eyes—
there is more to me than just the potency of my femininity.
You must earn your turn to occupy the privilege of being my lover
because I'm committed to God, myself, and no other.
So, we will not celebrate the beauty of this prize
before the appointed time.

—RM HARRIS

7

DON'T GIVE AWAY THE "PRIZE" PREMATURELY.

It is human nature to want to connect with someone on a physical level after we have romantically connected with them on a deep emotional level. However, when we make decisions based purely on emotion, we could be digging a hole for the expectations of our relationship that may be difficult to dig our way out of later in the relationship.

There are so many responsibilities that come along with sex that it can sometimes be overwhelming. Now, don't get me wrong, sex is great, but when done right there is so much more to consider than just performance and physical pleasures. There are many questions surrounding sex that we need to ask in order to determine whether or not Mr. Man, who's whispering in our ear, answers them in a way that satisfies us enough to give it up. When it comes to sex, we could be setting up unrealistic expectations or sacrificing a quality relationship in the name of fulfilling our physical needs too soon.

Infatuation is a strong motivator. In the beginning stages of a relationship, we see the good in our partner and are more willing to give the not-so-good the benefit of the doubt. Once that time is

GIRL LET GO OR BE DRAGGED

over and the shine wears off, there has to be something real, substantive, and concrete to continue to build upon. If the foundation was laid with sex, it may as well have been laid on sand. When we give too much too soon, we risk the other person falling in love with our hand instead of our heart.

I'm sure you've heard of the "90-Day Rule" that encourages us to steer clear of sex in the first three months of dating. Your metrics might vary depending on past experiences, religion, or other personal values. Whatever steers our decisions in the sexual arena, we must keep in mind that there are other ways to experience intimacy apart from sex. For many decades now, women have taken pride in exerting our sexual liberties in the name of equality, but this may be an area where being countercultural can benefit us tremendously. There are always exceptions, but generally, in the process of taking the time to really get to know our significant others, we increase our chances of forming strong, healthy bonds and discovering whether we have a true, reciprocated interest or a connection that isn't based primarily on sexual expectation. Having sex first and hoping to develop a relationship later potentially eliminates the opportunity to form an emotional or intellectual bond. Inadvertently, the relationship becomes just about the physical aspect. When this happens, we can cloud our judgment as to whether we and our love interests are even an appropriate match for each other. While not impossible, it does add a layer of complications because of the expectations that have already been set. Building an emotional connection first strengthens the relationship and gives clarity on what the relationship is about, giving us a better chance for a long-lasting union.

Additionally, there's something to be said for building up anticipation. In today's world of immediate gratification, we've forgotten that waiting awhile for what we want maximizes the pleasure of what's to come. Building anticipation gives us more opportunity for imagination and a greater appreciation once we've gotten what we desired, simply because we had to wait to get it. Inadvertently, waiting increases the significance and value of the anticipated moment, making it even more memorable. And if we realize after a few short interactions that we don't even like the person and things don't pan out, waiting keeps us from the regret and potential embarrassment of jumping in too soon. The decisions we make in relationships are heavily dependent on psychology, which gives us the tools to hack our minds for the greatest benefit.

If you taste all the food while it's still on the grill, what appetite will you have for dinner?

While we sometimes assume that for a man to take us seriously we need to show him that we care by giving up the "meow," that logic might be backfiring on us. Of course, men want sex. We all do—we're biological creatures. But if we move into the physical part of things prematurely, we might be sending the message that we don't want anything serious, in turn, causing our significant other to not take us seriously or consider us as potential long-term romantic partners. Having sex on the first or second date could send the impression that we're *just* looking for sex—nothing more.

Although this might not be the case, it's the message our actions may be giving. As always, communication is key, and as the experts say, nonverbal communication is more credible than verbal. If we have sex before having a serious conversation about it with the man we're dating, the only information he has to go on is what we're saying with our actions, and those actions set the expectation for future interactions. If we're looking for something deeper, we need to set a framework of what we're looking for by talking about those things in the order we want them to appear.

Having sex too early increases the likelihood of someone getting their feelings hurt, feeling confused about the nature or potential of the relationship, or putting pressure on the future expectations of the relationship. Talking about the physical aspect of things eliminates that confusion and sets a precedent of conversations about important matters as the standard in how you approach difficult topics. From the start, make a practice of communicating. Talk about what you're looking for at this stage in life and characteristics that make you compatible as a partner. If a prospect looks promising, take the time to get to know each other. A little more time on the front end could save us heartache on the back end. If you feel comfortable with them, the sex has the potential to be much more satisfying. Intellect, shared interest, and values are much stronger pillars to build a foundation on than sex, and when partners are aligned in these aspects, the sex has the potential to be exponentially more meaningful and fulfilling all the way around. I'm not saying to wait until you're married for sex, unless that's what you choose to do. I am saying that taking just a little bit of time to ensure you want this person in your life before going full throttle on the physical side can make a world of difference in your relationship, and even in your own personal health. When we get to know each other's minds, physical satisfaction follows. When we base everything on the physical, frustration is likely right around the corner. If our partner has challenges waiting, then maybe it's time to consider if we should let go or be dragged!

Don't give away the "Prize" prematurely. Waiting not only builds up the anticipation and inadvertently causes more appreciation, but it also tells us how we must remember our value. The Bible tells us in Proverbs 31 that our value is far above rubies, and we must overstand this!

Am I the girl for today, or for all your tomorrows?
Are we forever, or is a real future with you a never?
Do you see us with grandkids and growing old together?
Because that's how I see us, I see us as forever
Date me with respect, honor, and love
But date me with intentions and purpose
I'm dating with an end goal of forever
Because that's what I desire most above

—SHENISE

8

DOES HE SPEAK OF YOU IN HIS FUTURE PLANS?

It is important to notice what is being communicated, even in non-communication. If our partners are not generally speaking of us in their future plans, we may want to consider the possibility that they do not envision us in their future. If we are not considered in the long haul, it is time to question what exactly the relationship goals are, how significant is the union, and if we should be letting go to not get dragged! This could be especially challenging for us when it is someone we have a strong desire for. You can just see your future with him in your mind. Girl, you've been fantasizing about the house you'll share, cooking his food, coordinating outfits for family photos (you know them matching holiday onesies!), future vacation destinations, and so much more. You have thoroughly convinced yourself that this man is a great fit for you, but does he think you're a great fit for him? Hmmm . . . when we are the kind of women who believe in playing the long game, it is imperative that we find out if he is on the same page so that we are not wasting our time, energy, and resources on a relationship that is destined to stay right where it's at.

I know, this is a very sensitive topic, but certainly not one to be approached rashly. We may sometimes feel it is too early to bring it up in the beginning stages of a relationship, when really it is not. Have you ever thought to yourself, "Gosh, if I could just get an itty-bitty, teenie-weenie, tiny little hint, I would be alright!"? Trust me, we all have. What we may not realize is that the signs are usually there, but only if we're willing to see them. Before we'd ask a man anything about a future, we should have a talk with ourselves first to discover if we've possibly missed any hints he may have already given.

Playing the "H-Game"

Hypotheticals are what dreams are made of. They're the possibilities that keep our minds occupied when we're apart from our beau and help us push through the times in our relationships that aren't so sweet. Does your beau sometimes play the H-Game with you, where he is asking "what-if" questions like:

- "Ever thought about purchasing a home? If so, where do you envision yourself settling down?" Mansplained: I'd love to buy a home with you, and I hope we desire to live in the same town.
- "Would you elope if ever you decided to get married?" Mansplained: Does she want to get married? What type of wedding would she like?

◆ "What if you got a chance to move to Miami, would you go?"
  Mansplained: I like you so much and wonder if you would
  just up and leave me.

If so, a future together is unquestionably on his mind. Absolutely, he's trying to get to know you, but he is also trying to see how your future would mesh with his. Men sometimes think they're being subtle when really, they aren't. If they're asking us questions about the future, especially concerning major life choices, that means they're probably trying to see if the feeling is mutual. But if his conversations rarely go past the weekend plans, you might be the girl for him "today," but not so much "tomorrow."

Me or We?

Little words can have big implications. Is your beau's language inclusive of you, or is it focused on him alone? When he talks about the picture of the future he sees for himself, are you in that Polaroid too? It might be something to be concerned about if he is suggesting opportunities that do not take you into consideration, like the following examples:

◆ "I think it would be cool if my job sent me overseas."
◆ "I like that motorcycle, but I especially like the ones that go
  faster."
◆ "I want to live in that house."

Or does he suggest opportunities that take you into consideration, like:

- "If my job sent me overseas, would you be down to visit or go with me?"
- "Motorcycles are cool, but I wouldn't want you to be worried about me, especially on the ones that go superfast."
- "I'd love to raise our family in that house."

Even in his short-term plans, if he's telling you what he's going to do instead of inviting you into the thought or planning process, like, "I'm going to Vegas for Christmas," instead of, "I'd like for us to go to Vegas for Christmas," pay attention. He doesn't need to involve you all the time; we all need our space. But you do want to be aware of whether you're a first thought, an afterthought, or a thought at all.

He Talks About the Future You . . .

If he makes comments about the future you, he's clearly considering making big plans with you in them. Does he comment that you'd make a beautiful bride or a wonderful mother? Whether he says it in passing or in a moment of focus and intention, understand that men don't throw those sacred words around unprompted unless it's really on their mind.

. . . And He Wonders How Your Future Might Affect Him

Does your beau seem a little more concerned about the decisions you make than a casual friend would? That might be because he's thinking about how your decisions will affect him later. If it made no difference to him, he would only go so far with advice about your career path, financial decisions, state of health, or other facets of your life that will have long-term consequences. If what happens to you will spill over to him later, he'll be more willing to help you think through difficult situations and encourage you to challenge yourself more.

When we're ready for big steps in our lives, there's no need to spend time with someone who isn't ready for the next steps in his life, too. No matter how fun, handsome, or well-adjusted they are, it's important to understand whether their future long-term plans align with ours. We should tune our ears to the nuances of our significant others' conversations to deduce whether they're having the same daydreams we are. If it becomes clear that they're not in it for the long haul, it's time to reconsider whether the relationship is one we find value in continuing to pursue. There's no need to waste today with men who have no interest in inviting us into their tomorrow.

Does he speak of you in his future plans? We should understand that if a man imagines us in his future we will know; he will not hesitate to tell us his endgame. The man God has for us will mirror the same adoration and love God shows us. Jerimiah 29:11 says, "I know the thoughts that I have for you . . . plans to an expected end."

Hide-and-go-seek is for the kids and the clowns
Yet I feel like you hide me so we could never be found—out
By your family, friends, and even ya foes,
Because in real life I want the whole world to know
About the love I believe that we share,
But as of late I'm starting to wonder if it's even really there

—SHENISE

9

DOES HE HIDE YOU?

It's normal to want to have a sense of surety before bringing our significant other around the people we care about the most. We don't want to give the impression that something is more serious than it really is or risk attachments for someone who isn't going to be around long-term. If a man is giving the impression that things are serious, but a good stretch into the relationship he hasn't introduced his woman to any family or friends, or he's not up to going out in public with her very often, this is a red flag. It might mean he's trying to hide the relationship, and it may be time to let go or be dragged! Consider these reasons why a man might want to keep a relationship under wraps:

- ◆ **He wants to keep his options open.**
  Maybe the woman he's with is *kind of* what he wants but doesn't check all the boxes. If this is the case, and he feels like he's settling, he might be hiding the relationship because he wants to seem available to the dating pool. It's plausible that there's one person in particular he's keeping his fingers crossed for, like an ex, or a crush he's wanted in the past who didn't return his feelings. It could be as simple

as he likes attention from other women. No matter the motivation, if we don't agree to sneaky link arrangements, it's unfair to force us into restrictions that make us feel insecure about the relationship. Additionally, if any of the above is the case, it's reasonable to assume he may cheat as soon as the opportunity presents itself.

Unless we've agreed to an open relationship, there's nothing cool about a man behaving like he's single or available. If significant others are keeping us private, then it's time to question what THEY are doing in private. While we're being loyal "good girls," they're out there swiping right on dating apps!

◆ **He's only keeping you around for the short term.**
If a man feels (or knows!) a relationship is a short-term situation, why would he flaunt it? That would open the door to lots of questions that he would not want to answer when things end. It's easier to have fun now and not have to explain anything later. Think about what would happen if he made things public, people got excited, then you started posting to social media, and now you all are #couplegoals. Right? Then, when things end prematurely, that would be public too.

No one wants the burden of explaining why the relation-ship ended so soon, having to delete all the photos from

SHENISE TRUESDELL

social media, and picking up the pieces of your life in public (in front of family and friends too). So, if he knows he's not keeping you around for the long haul, chances are he won't make your relationship public—simple as that.

◆ **He thinks he can do better.**
Sometimes, men will use women to fill a void until they find someone who they think is better. This is often referred to as the "Bigger Better Deal" (BBD). If he believes he can do better, then maybe he's keeping the girl of the day as a placeholder until "Miss Right" comes along.

If a woman does not measure up to a guy's perfect ideal future woman, he may not be proud to be seen with her in public. There may be some qualities about her that he likes or will settle with for the time being. He may like what she does for him, and or how she makes him feel, but it is not enough for him to make it official and introduce her to loved ones, or even take her out in public often.

◆ **He might have someone else.**
Are you ready for a hard truth? If we are in a committed relationship and our man is hiding us, there very well might be another woman or other women. If this is the case, realize there's no good way this thing ends, so the sooner

it ends, the better. Being a side piece or part of a player's team makes us feel deceived, second-rate, taken advantage of, and used. It's a terrible feeling that no one wants to ever experience, especially when we gave no permission to be a part of it in the first place. Now our feelings are involved, and worst-case scenario, we could be in danger. No man is worth the headache and heartache that come along with trying to untangle such a mess.

If a man is hiding us because we're not the only one, there will be other signs. We must pay attention to their habits, schedules, and long absences in addition to avoiding being seen with us in certain places. If it wasn't our choice to be the other woman or one of many, we should never let it be our choice to remain in that entanglement.

The reality is, he's not ready for a monogamous relationship, and he's probably the guy who desires to have his cake, and ice cream, and sprinkles, and whipped cream, and cherry toppings, and chocolate syrup . . . you get my drift. These types of men can be described as serial cheaters, and it takes a while for them to change their ways, if ever. This level of deception is unacceptable and speaks directly to the character of that person. *¡No bueno!*

After dating this one guy for a while, Jazzy felt things were starting to get pretty serious between them. Her family thought he was great and had even given him an approval. Jazzy wanted to meet his family and friends as well, and often expressed her wish to him, but she understood that maybe the relationship needed more maturing before meeting his loved ones, so she acquiesced on the matter. Another thing that was starting to bother Jazzy was the fact that he never really took her on dates. After a while, she was over it! She was not willing to forgo this, so she had a conversation with him about it, and he obliged. They were out nearly every other weekend, and Jazzy could not have been any happier. It was just one thing she'd realized: Their dates were always far out, usually in a neighboring city or county. Jazzy brought it to his attention, and after stumbling over his words, he responded with an excuse that did not make any sense. This made Jazzy very leery of him, to the point that she started to rethink their relationship. Regrettably, against her better judgment, she did not end their relationship, and about a year later, she discovered he was not the person she thought he was. Turns out, her guy was very popular, a well-known player, a man with many women in Atlanta to be exact, and with a very disturbing past. This explains why at the beginning of the relationship, he never brought her around his loved ones, and why he took her on dates outside of the city. Jazzy was well within her rights to question him about her concerns. Was this an indication that he may have been hiding her (or himself, for that matter!)? Either way, it was certainly giving dubious energy, which was a huge red flag. In this case, Jazzy did not let go and unfortunately, was dragged.

Does he hide you? Hiding is fear of being seen. Is your partner in fear of being seen with you? There is no room in love for fear. Well-formed love banishes fear, not you. 1 John 4:18 says, "There is no fear in love. But perfect love drives out fear..."

Love, self-love, and all the things.
If love is never given to us, then do we really have it?
If we don't have it, then how can we give it?

—SHENISE

10

IF HE DOESN'T LOVE AND VALUE HIMSELF, CAN HE TRULY LOVE AND VALUE YOU?

You know the saying, "You can't give what you don't have"? That applies to almost everything in life, including time, money, and love. When dealing with partners who have low self-esteem and struggle to love themselves, we can bet they'll have trouble loving us too. Love starts from within. If someone lacks it, they can't genuinely give it. If we spend our energy trying to help others heal if they're not ready, we must be careful that they don't tear us down while we're trying to build them up. Pay attention to the red flags that scream a man struggles with his self-worth.

He loves to see you suffer.

We know by now that hurting people hurt people. Even when we treat someone with love and fairness, we can't assume they'll return the gesture. If a man is unhappy with himself, if he is in pain or dealing with past trauma, he might enjoy seeing his woman suffer in the relationship. Sick, huh? If this feels far-fetched, trust me—it's not. It happens all the time, and sometimes before we even realize what's going on. A damaged heart can be a dangerous thing. If our romantic partner's self-esteem gets so low that they would feel validated when we suffer or when we are experiencing the pain that they've caused, it may be a boost to their ego. That quick hit of power when realizing they can get us to step away from our character can be like a drug to them. Misery loves company, so sometimes the more someone tears us down, the more empowered they feel. Ladies, if this is the case in your relationship, we must remember that we are much more than someone's cheap high at the expense of our pain. Love doesn't have to hurt to be genuine. If we realize this is the situation we are in, we need to let go!

He's jealous or insecure.

Actress Julie Walters said, "Self-worth is everything. Without it, life is misery," and she was right. A low sense of self-worth doesn't just make life miserable for the person who lacks confidence, but also for everyone around them. A man who lacks confidence reeks of insecurity, becomes jealous easily, and is ill-equipped to adequately love us or embrace our love for them. Before their unsuspecting partner knows it, they've made her their entire support system, but they don't show appreciation, and if they feel threatened by any outside force that might take precedence over them for even a moment, they can't handle it.

A feeling of self-worth impacts every single part of our lives: how we treat ourselves, how we treat our loved ones, what we think we can achieve, how we treat strangers, how we deal with hard times, how we deal with good times—literally everything. Men with low self-esteem might make us feel great before we realize they don't think much of themselves since they need to win us over to fill the void within themselves. Once they've showered us with compliments and notions of how awesome we are (and we are, but motive makes all the difference) and we've gotten emotionally involved, feeling like we're the best thing that's ever happened to them (because we very well might be), then the real "him" may finally come out. We won't like it. We'll try to leave. They'll become irrational. If we leave, they'll feel empty again. They might straighten up for a little while, but authenticity always wins. Always. The cycle will go on and on. In fact, they can't explain why they do the things they do, but this behavior is normal for people who don't love themselves. A lack of self-love has got to be painful, painful enough for some to want to make others feel the same level of pain they're experiencing. Ironically, when something good comes along, they feel uncomfortable because they believe they aren't truly deserving of anything good. In many cases, these types of men think we'd leave them for someone else, someone "better," and if so, it will only confirm that they were right in believing they were never good enough in the first place. So, they avail themselves of other women or relationships to soften the blow in case we decide to leave them.

He may seek attention outside the relationship or in activities without you.

Men with major insecurities and low self-esteem have the reputation of being serial cheaters. They crave attention from anywhere. Any woman who approves them, validates them, flirts, or throws come hither looks their way opens the potential for infidelity. Dating sites or apps? Gold mines. They'll bend over backward for the smallest dose of attention because the attention they get from us isn't enough. It is like a drop of water into a bucket. When it comes to who will look their way, the more the merrier. Lack of self-esteem is an impossible hole to fill. Without doing the work from within, no number of admirers could ever do the job.

Having low self-esteem is like looking in a dirty mirror. We can only see tainted reflections of ourselves, but we can never see ourselves in full. Our true self can't shine through all the blemishes. When all that's visible is damaged, cleaning it up can seem over-whelming. If our partner can't see who he is because he hasn't healed from whatever stifled his emotional growth, we should try to talk to him about it. Pointed questions like the following can help him get to the underlying issue of his behavior:

- I think you act like this because of how it makes you feel. How *does* it make you feel?
- Why do you need to feel this way?
- Why do you feel like you can't just be yourself?
- Why am I not enough? Why do you need validation from others?
- Do you need help learning how to love yourself?

If he can't handle such a conversation, he's not ready for growth or maturity. The will to change must be his own; it is NEVER your responsibility to shoulder this weight for him.

Even the healthiest relationships have their share of challenges. There's no need to compound those challenges by sticking with someone who simply isn't ready to grow in health together. If your man's self-esteem is a problem, it's not your problem, so girl, let go or be dragged!

Simon, who is a recently single man, dated his ex-girlfriend for nearly two years before the relationship ended. He recounts how their relationship was very rocky almost from the start and that he was mainly to blame. Simon admits that due to his challenges with being overweight, he was not happy with himself. His ex was an extremely intelligent and strikingly attractive woman, so that didn't help the situation at all, because he often felt especially intimidated by her beauty. He described the moments he'd say things to make her question her looks or attack her self-esteem simply because she appeared too secure. He said this behavior normally occurred after she'd groom herself when they were getting ready to go out together, or even when she'd go out with friends. Simon considers himself a reformed womanizer who used to struggle with extremely low self-esteem to get what he wanted. He attributes his behavior toward his ex-girlfriend to his battle to truly love himself. He mentions how she was a great, supportive woman and that he fears he may have damaged her because he was unhealed and in denial throughout their entire relationship.

Simon thought the day would never come, but it did. She mustered up the courage to leave him one final time. Although Simon said he was very heartbroken that she eventually left him, after completing the self-work, he can appreciate the pain of their split. He feels that it was the pain of the break-up that empowered him to do some introspection and ultimately arrive to the healed version of himself he is proud to be today.

How often do we hear of these types of stories? Unfortunately, this is very typical, and sadly so when couples get married or have children, which makes things even more difficult. Simon's ex stayed for almost two years, but at some point, she loved herself enough to leave that toxic situation. Her deciding to let go and not be dragged not only saved her, but it helped him become a better man.

Does he have low self-esteem? If he doesn't value himself, can he truly value you? What does the Bible say about he who finds a wife has found a good thing? A good thing is a thing of true value. Strive to be a Proverbs 31 woman, a virtuous woman, because we are of true value, and should feel valued by our partner under any and all circumstances.

You see, in a relationship, you, my dear sister, are responsible for
speaking up when your partner is projecting foolishness.
Address things that you see immediately,
because this will save you time, heartache, pain, and energy.
When you hold your partner accountable, you will see
your relationship atmosphere become stable
Being proactive verses reactive is the best remedy
to combat lies and fables.
Long gone are the days of you pointing your finger at the man
Because it's time for you to take a firm stand
A stand that speaks of your willingness not to allow unscrupulous
behavior to go unchecked
And your emotional needs to go unmet.

—RM HARRIS

11

TAKE RESPONSIBILITY FOR THE UNACCEPTABLE BEHAVIOR YOU ALLOW AND HAVE ACCEPTED IN THE RELATIONSHIP. OWN YOUR PART!

Responsibility is a big word. For us to be happy and whole, we must take responsibility for our decisions and demand respectful treatment from our loved ones. Likewise, if we want to cultivate healthy relationships, we need to be involved with a significant other who listens, takes responsibility for their actions, and adjusts accordingly. When we notice behavior that we're not willing to accept, and we shed light on the matter, if our men hear us and make the necessary changes, they're proving they are men of respect who are ready for serious relationships. On the other hand, if they argue, claim they didn't do what we said they did, justify their disrespect, or otherwise diminish our feelings, it's time to take a closer look and examine if this is where we belong.

At the start of relationships, the tendency is to overlook bad behaviors. At the very least, we're often so consumed with infatuation, we may not even notice character flaws. The problem with this is if we don't address bad behavior at the start, our significant others will get comfortable because they'll think we think it's okay. In this way, we contribute to our own misery. Infatuation is fun; there's nothing like it. There's something to be said for the newness and exploration phase of a relationship, but maturity requires us to get ahold of ourselves enough to notice the potholes that can become pitfalls later. If we keep quiet in the name of trying to "be his peace," we will quickly destroy any peace we could have within ourselves. If you're wondering what behaviors to watch out for, read on.

◆ **They hurt your feelings on purpose.**
There's no way to completely avoid hurt feelings in a relationship. Sooner or later, we won't see eye to eye with our significant other, something won't go the way we would have liked, and our emotions will take a hit. It's natural. Sometimes, our man will inadvertently hurt our feelings. Other times, we will inadvertently hurt their feelings. When this happens, the offending party needs to swallow their pride and make things right with a willingness to see the other person's point of view. However, sadly, these instances aren't accidents in every relationship. There are people out there who *want* to hurt us. They want to make us feel small to make themselves seem powerful. A person who needs to make others feel inferior so they can feel superior is a person who has too much inner work to do to try to be in a relationship with anybody else.

When we live in a state of potential emotional attack, we can't be vulnerable. If we live in fear of being hurt by someone who's supposed to care for us, we can't be ourselves. If we can't be ourselves in a relationship, what are we doing there?

◆ **They don't offer support when you need it.**

One reason humans seek out relationships is because life is both hard and beautiful. When life is hard, we need support to get through rough spots. When life is beautiful, we want someone to celebrate with us and recognize the hard work that's earned us the accolades we deserve. If our significant other can't offer that support, they will quickly become extra weight we're carrying while trying to carry ourselves through the various seasons of life.

There may be several reasons a significant other won't offer support. They might be emotionally closed off from having had to deal with trauma in their own lives. They might feel "self-made" and think since they didn't need anyone to cheer them on down the road to achievement, other folks don't either. Sometimes, believe it or not, they might be jealous of our success, fearing that if we attain too much, we'll leave them behind. None of these issues is our problem or responsibility. Those issues should be between that person and their therapist. We do not have to take on other people's issues. If they can't offer support, they'll be an annoyance at best and a hindrance at worst. Don't subject yourself to this misery. Walk away.

◆ **They don't listen to you.**
One of the first actions we ever perform as humans, unless we are impaired, is listening. Babies know their parents' voices at birth because they've been listening to those voices in the womb. Before we talk, we need to listen so we'll know what sounds to imitate and how to build our vocabulary. Teachers give lectures, preachers give sermons, and singers give concerts because we listen. But despite how natural it is to do so, many people are still terrible at it because they don't see it as the powerful skill it is.

Communication is everything. There's a reason why the oldest and most repetitive advice to any functional relationship almost always revolves around listening. If your significant other doesn't show interest in what you have to say, if they think your thoughts are unimportant, or they just ignore you, hoping you'll eventually stop talking, your most basic human need is not being met. Just as bad as being ignored is being stonewalled. When used as a precursor for abuse, the silent treatment can leave the victim feeling hurt, powerless, invisible, guilty, and frustrated. Listening is a small action that speaks volumes. Make sure you're paying attention.

- **You've caught them lying.**

  Yes, the big lies are heartbreaking. Cheating, stealing, excessive gambling, or other secrets have tremendous effects that are hard to heal from. But the small lies can be just as harmful, like death by a million cuts.

  Small lies chip away at trust and show a lack of respect for the relationship. If the other party in the relationship can't be bothered to be honest, what evidence do you have that you should continue to trust them?

- **They don't prioritize you.**

  We know what it feels like to be a priority. We also know what it feels like when we're an afterthought.

  When we're a priority, the other person will move mountains to be around us, to help us when we need it, and to take our needs and wants into consideration. But when we're not, the other person will be distracted when they're around us, change or cancel plans often and for no reason, chronically show up late for dates, and prioritize friends and work over us. In a relationship, if you have to beg for attention, think about what that means and respond accordingly.

  It is very possible for "good" people to display behaviors that make them seem not so good, but remember, you don't have to stick around and wait for somebody to get themselves together, especially since sometimes, they never do.

Oftentimes in our relationships we'll notice the flaws of our partners without truly recognizing our own. Even though we may not have intentionally committed any offenses against our partners, we must not be of the mindset that we are perfect and without fault in the failing relationship. Matthew 7:3 says, "Why do you see the speck that is in your brother's eye, but don't consider the beam that is in your own eye?"

CONCLUSION

As relational beings, we're all searching for the right person to spend our time with, and maybe even to spend the rest of our lives with. There's nothing wrong with that. However, we all have different motives, backgrounds, and experiences that shape how we approach the search. When we feel like time is running out, we're behind where we thought we'd be in life by now, or our standards are too high, it becomes all too easy to overlook the signs that tell us when *a* person is not *the* person and that we should keep waiting and looking.

Part of loving ourselves is keeping ourselves out of harm's way. We have the power to save ourselves a world of heartache if we take the wisdom and experiences of those who are willing to share their truth with us instead of making every mistake for ourselves. A willingness to listen and apply others' wisdom to our own situations saves our emotional pain, embarrassing explanations, time, and money. All that energy can be put into further building our careers, friendships, and other relationships. All these things can also bring fulfillment. But when we put those resources into a toxic, dead-end relationship, we will see no return on our investment.

Choosing the right partner comes down to three things: trusting ourselves, trusting the advice of those who want the best for us, and trusting the timing is right. It might take a while, but isn't waiting for the right person a better bet than rushing the wrong one in to disrupt an otherwise carefully curated life?

Making decisions from a place of self-love is what this book encourages, and it is for two main reasons: to guard our hearts and to protect the parts of our lives that are indeed worthy of protection. This may be professional progress, our children, other family members, mental health—anything we count as valuable. The wrong person will disrupt all those things, and once the damage is done, it's hard to undo and even harder to forget. When we're not sure what to believe about a significant other, we must believe what's in front of us, examine their personal relationships, and pay attention to how they speak to us and how they speak about others. Give it enough time, look with honest eyes, listen to how their loved ones speak of them, and know the truth will always reveal itself.

While we're waiting for the clarity we seek, it is vital that we hold out on giving away every part of ourselves. The connections sex creates are usually difficult to break if things end badly or prematurely. Remember that most men usually flaunt what they're proud of, so if they're hiding us, they may not be proud of having us around. Remember that no man who doesn't love himself can love anyone else appropriately. Anyone who cannot love themselves may not be equipped to fulfill the role of a partner. And finally, if we're wondering if they're weaving us into their plans now and forever, it's important for us to ask ourselves if we even want that person in our own plans that long. No man is worth the sacrifice of a life well-built unless they are, and if they are, they need to consistently prove that on every front. However, if there is any inkling to believe they are not, then it is time to let go or be dragged—don't play yourself!

Finally, always remember, who we spend our lives with is a choice. With choice comes responsibility. Our responsibility is to be sure that when we're saying yes to someone else, we're not saying no to ourselves.

I'm Grateful for Your Purchase!

As A Token of My Appreciation - Scan the QR Code
for a Free Gift from Me to You with Love!

Let's Keep In Touch!

Follow Me on Instagram!

@GIRL.LET.GO